Making Art

Erica Smith

Rosen REAL READERS

Rosen Classroom Books and Materials
New York

Published in 2002 by The Rosen Publishing Group, Inc.
29 East 21st Street, New York, NY 10010

Book Design: Haley Wilson

Photo Credits: Cover, pp. 1, 5 © Danny Lehman/Corbis; p. 5 © W. Cody/ Corbis/Nicole Katano/International Stock/Scott Barrow/International Stock; p. 6 © Franz-Marc Frei/Corbis; pp. 8, 9 © Zefa Visual Media-Germany/ Scott Barrow/International Stock; p. 11 © Michael Ventura/International Stock; p. 13 © Corbis; p. 14 © Bill Tucker/International Stock.

ISBN: 0-8239-8217-3
6-pack ISBN: 0-8239-8620-9

Manufactured in the United States of America

Contents

What Is Art?

People make art using tools and their **imagination**. There are many different kinds of art. Some people paint pictures, draw, or take pictures with a **camera**. Other people make shapes out of clay or rock. People can use computers to make art, too.

People use many different tools to create art. ▷

Painting

This man is a painter. He uses brushes and colored paints to make pictures. Some of his paintings come from his imagination. Others are pictures of things he sees around him. This painter likes to paint pictures of mountains.

◁ Painting on a canvas is one way for a person to use his or her imagination.

Sculpting

A sculptor makes art using clay, rock, wood, or metal. **Sculptures** can be seen  in parks, gardens, buildings, and homes. Sculptures can take any shape or form. They can be very large or very small.

Some sculptures help us remember heroes and events of the past. We call these sculptures **monuments**.

Sculptures of people can be much larger than life! The Lincoln Memorial is located in Washington, D.C. It is nineteen feet tall.

This sculpture is called the Unisphere. It is in Flushing, New York. It was built for the 1964–1965 New York World's Fair.

9

Drawing and Designing

Many children like to draw. Grown-ups like to draw, too. Some grown-ups even work at jobs that let them draw all day long!

Think of a picture book that you really like. An **illustrator** drew all of the pictures that appear in the book. A **designer** used a computer to put the pictures and words together in a way that is easy to read and looks interesting.

Do you like to draw and work on a computer? If you do, you may have a job designing books someday.

Taking Photographs

Photography is the art of taking pictures with a camera. Tools such as special lights can help a **photographer** do his or her job.

Photographs appear in magazines and books. Photographs are also in art **museums**. Any person can get a camera and take photographs.

Some people make their livings as photographers.

You Can Make Art

You have just read about many kinds of art that people can make. Some forms of art will be new to you. It is fun to try them!

You can paint a picture with colorful paints. Ask a grown-up to help you find a camera and take photographs. Your art teacher can help you make a sculpture out of clay. Making art is fun!

Glossary

camera A machine used for taking pictures.

designer A person who uses a computer to put words and pictures together.

illustrator A person who draws pictures for books.

imagination The ideas and dreams in your mind.

monument Something set up to honor a person or an event.

museum A building where art or historical objects are kept for people to see.

photographer A person who takes pictures with a camera.

photography The art of taking pictures with a camera.

sculpture A form made out of clay, rock, wood, or metal.

Index